INNOVATIVE TECHNOLOGIES

SUSTAINABLE AGRICULTURE

ABDO
Publishing Company

INNOVATIVE TECHNOLOGIES

SUSTAINABLE AGRICULTURE

BY LISA OWINGS

CONTENT CONSULTANT

Ryan Anderson

Assistant Professor, Agricultural Education and Studies

Iowa State University

CREDITS

Published by ABDO Publishing Company, PO Box 398166, Minneapolis, MN 55439. Copyright © 2013 by Abdo Consulting Group, Inc. International copyrights reserved in all countries. No part of this book may be reproduced in any form without written permission from the publisher. The Essential Library™ is a trademark and logo of ABDO Publishing Company.

Printed in the United States of America,
North Mankato, Minnesota

092012
012013

 THIS BOOK CONTAINS AT LEAST 10% RECYCLED MATERIALS.

Editor: Melissa York
Series Designer: Craig Hinton

Photo Credits: Shutterstock Images, cover, 12, 40, 76; Sam Dcruz/Shutterstock Images, 6; Dudarev Mikhail/Shutterstock Images, 9; Gregory A. Harlin/National Geographic/Heritage Images, 14; DEA Picture Library/De Agostini/Getty Images, 16; Alain Lauga/Shutterstock Images, 19; AP Images, 20; Dr. Morely Read/Shutterstock Images, 22; NASA, 27; Elena Elisseeva/Shutterstock Images, 30; Red Line Editorial, 33; Nate A./Shutterstock Images, 34; Martin D. Vonka/Shutterstock Images, 37; AZP Worldwide/Shutterstock Images, 43; Frank Zeller/AFP/Getty Images, 48; Alida Vanni/iStockphoto, 52; Ceasar Maragni/The Southern Illinoisan/AP Images, 54; Joel Page/AP Images, 60; Vicki Reid/iStockphoto, 64; Alfred de Montesquiou/AP Images, 68; Michigan State University/AP Images, 71; Carrie Antlfinger/AP Images, 75; David Jennings/AP Images, 79; John Wollwerth/Shutterstock Images, 82; Nickolay Stanev/Shutterstock Images, 85; Hemera Technologies/Thinkstock, 88; Dmitry Berkut/Shutterstock Images, 90; Gary Kazanjian/AP Images, 92; Doug Berry/iStockphoto, 97; Seth Wenig/AP Images, 100

Library of Congress Cataloging-in-Publication Data
Owings, Lisa.
   Sustainable agriculture / Lisa Owings.
      p. cm. -- (Innovative technologies)
   Includes bibliographical references.
   ISBN 978-1-61783-468-4
1. Sustainable agriculture. I. Title. II. Series: Innovative technologies.
S494.5.S86O95 2013
631.5--dc23
                        2012023992

>> TABLE OF
CONTENTS

FOOD FOR THOUGHT

Approximately 7 billion people call our planet home. That number continues to grow at a rate of just over 1 percent per year.[1] All of these billions of people, now and in the future, need enough food to live and be healthy. Providing enough food for everyone is putting a strain on Earth's resources. Practicing sustainable agriculture means looking for solutions that conserve resources and preserve the land for the future.

WHAT IS AGRICULTURE?

Agriculture is the practice of growing crops, raising livestock, growing or caring for forests, and raising or catching fish. The most important product of agriculture is food. However, agriculture also provides many other products and services. It provides important sources of fiber and fuel, such as wool and wood. It also provides natural

« Farming is practiced worldwide, as in these rice and other fields in Uganda.

chemicals used in medicines and other products. Agriculture is an important source of plant and animal genes. Scientists study these genes and use the information they gather to improve agriculture and create new kinds of plants and animals. Agriculture can even supply people with fresh, clean water.

Not only does agriculture provide vital foods, products, and services, but it also has the potential to help solve some of the major problems the world faces. It can keep people healthier and reduce health-care costs. It can also create job opportunities and improve people's quality of life. Approximately 40 percent of people worldwide make their living primarily in agriculture, and by some measures, approximately 40 percent of Earth's land is devoted to agriculture.[2] Without agriculture, life as we know it would never have been possible.

A SUSTAINABLE SOLUTION

A sustainable system can keep going long term. It conserves natural resources so others will be able to use those resources in the future. The goal of sustainable agriculture is to come up with ways of meeting the world's current agricultural needs without making it more difficult for future generations to do the same. At the same time, any sustainable agriculture system must work with and even enhance the land and the animal and plant species living in and around it. This means developing ways of farming that maintain harmony with the environment, make profits

Agriculture includes
raising livestock for food
and other products.

for farmers, and meet the needs of local and global communities. In the end, a sustainable agriculture system must have the responsibility for caring for the land and the surrounding environment built into it.

Despite recent advances in technology, agriculture is still dependent on the land. If a system of agriculture harms the land on and around which we grow our food, then that land may eventually be unable to support crops or livestock. Additionally, if farmers cannot make money by growing food, they will be forced to seek other work. Finally, if agriculture does not meet the needs of communities by providing people with high-quality food, rich cultural traditions, and satisfying jobs, communities will not support their farmers. Without the support of the

RECENT EVENTS IN SUSTAINABLE AGRICULTURE

2009: At the World Summit on Food Security in Rome, Italy, world leaders renewed their pledge to feed the world's hungry through sustainable agriculture.

2009: To celebrate the twentieth anniversary of Slow Food, an organization dedicated to good food grown sustainably, people in 120 countries participated in the movement toward diversity and sustainability in agriculture.

2009: After a decade of increased emissions, carbon dioxide emissions fell 1.3 percent worldwide, according to researchers in Germany.

2010: Approximately 60 countries agreed to spend more than $4 billion over three years to take steps toward reducing emissions from deforestation and forest degradation.

2010: Researchers said providing farmers in Africa with varieties of corn that grow well during droughts could increase yields by up to 25 percent by 2016.[3]

community, farming cannot be profitable. Thus, agriculture cannot be sustainable if it fails in any one of these areas. And meanwhile it must also work with nature, not against it.

One of the biggest challenges we face in developing a system of sustainable agriculture is that the natural world is constantly changing. We are experiencing major changes in Earth's climate, causing unpredictable and extreme weather that can wipe out crops. Many agricultural practices introduce toxic chemicals and foreign species into our environments, causing perpetual shifts in those ecosystems. We are also damaging our planet's biodiversity and depleting its natural resources, so nature must continually try to heal itself.

Every action we perform on the farm or in the grocery store has consequences that ripple outward. As these ripples spread into our

"Agricultural sustainability . . . asks, how can we equitably meet the needs of people in the present, while leaving equal or better opportunities for those of the future—not just how can we make food quick, convenient, and cheap? It asks, how can we develop an agriculture that is ecologically sound, economically viable, and socially responsible—not just how can we make agriculture more economically efficient? . . . Sustainability asks how can we sustain a desirable quality of human life on this earth, individually, socially, and ethically—both for ourselves and for those of future generations?"[4]

—*John E. Ikerd, professor emeritus of agricultural and applied economics, University of Missouri*

world, nature makes constant adjustments to bring itself back into balance. For many of these issues, a temporary solution that is only applied when a problem strikes will not be enough. As Joseph Fiksel, director of the Center for Resilience at Ohio State University, argues, systematic change will be necessary to solve these problems in a sustainable way.[5] A sustainable system of agriculture must be flexible enough to adapt to constant changes in nature. The human economic system is part of the planet's greater ecosystem, and a sustainable future will mean adapting our economic system to work within the limits of the ecosystem.

Many farmers around the world are up to the challenge of making agriculture sustainable. One of the major concerns producers are facing is the heavy use of fossil fuels in agriculture. Today, fossil fuels are heavily used for everything from transportation to generating heat and power. The total supply of fossil fuels on Earth is limited, and they will run out if we continue to use them. Any system that relies on fossil fuels cannot be sustainable. Some researchers and farmers are using technologies and techniques that decrease their use of fossil fuels to delay the problem in the short term. Others are working toward truly sustainable solutions that will carry us forward. Today, many innovative technologies and practices are transforming the future of agriculture.

« **Farming combines new and old technology.**

THE HISTORY OF AGRICULTURE

Humans existed for thousands of years without growing their own food. The earliest humans were all hunter-gatherers. They hunted and fished for meat, and they gathered edible plants and seeds from their wild surroundings. When food in one area became scarce, they moved to another area where food was more plentiful. By moving in small groups with few mouths to feed, they could stay in one place a bit longer.

THE RISE OF AGRICULTURE

The first signs of agriculture appeared between 10,000 and 15,000 years ago. Ancient cultures across the globe developed agriculture independently from one another. As a result, these people were able to harvest more food from a smaller area of land. They did not need to travel as often to find food, and their small groups grew larger as their

 Early humans hunted and gathered for survival.

Ancient Egyptians
harvesting grains

food supplies became more stable. Most crops grown by these early farmers were grains, such as barley, rye, and early forms of wheat.

As people's dependence on agriculture increased, they developed new tools, techniques, and technologies to help them grow and prepare food. As people traveled from place to place, these agricultural practices spread over the globe. As agriculture spread, settled life became more common. People established small villages, sometimes traveling to larger towns.

Innovation was constant. By the seventh century CE, most crops, livestock, and basic agricultural tools were similar to those used today.

INDUSTRIAL AGRICULTURE AND THE GREEN REVOLUTION

The biggest changes in agriculture began in the eighteenth century, just prior to the Industrial Revolution. People began using powered machines and chemical fertilizers and pesticides. By the early twentieth century, industrialized agriculture was widespread in Europe and North America. It was recognized as an efficient way to produce large quantities of food. Researchers also began studying plant and animal genes, which allowed them to breed improved crops and livestock.

Technological advances during the first half of the twentieth century served to make

NEW TECHNOLOGY: THE COTTON GIN

In the United States in the eighteenth century, cotton was widely grown for making fabric. To be spun into yarn, cotton had to be free of seeds. The process of removing the seeds, however, was a slow and labor-intensive process. Eli Whitney resolved this problem by inventing the cotton gin. This machine quickly removed cottonseeds by feeding the cotton through a comb with teeth set closer than the width of the seeds. The success of the cotton gin led to a huge increase in the amount of cotton grown, especially in the southern United States.

GREGOR MENDEL AND GENETICS

Gregor Mendel is widely considered to be the father of modern genetics. Through experiments in the nineteenth century, he discovered how traits—such as eye color in humans, flower color in plants, and disease resistance in animals—are transferred from parents to offspring. He also noted that certain traits are dominant over others. Mendel published his work in his home country of Austria, but his findings were largely ignored. He died before the importance of his work was recognized. In 1900, Mendel's work was rediscovered by a trio of scientists who appreciated its value. Since then, genetics has proved to be one of the most important branches of science and has given rise to a number of life-saving products.

industrial agriculture even more efficient. Gasoline-powered tractors allowed farmers to cultivate more land faster and with fewer workers than previous methods. Specialized machines for spraying pesticides and harvesting crops also decreased the labor needed for farming. The use of cars, trucks, and planes for transporting or applying agricultural products was another major shift in the early twentieth century. In addition to these new machines, crops such as soybeans, sorghum, and sugar beets began to be widely grown in Europe and North America during this time. Globally, farmers irrigated more of their land, increasing food production.

Also at the beginning of the twentieth century, researchers made new discoveries about how characteristics of plants and animals are passed from generation to generation

The threshing machine was invented in the eighteenth century.

and why different plants and animals inherit different characteristics. These discoveries were the foundation of the science of genetics. The new knowledge of genetics led scientists in technologically advanced nations to develop new varieties of important crops by breeding for certain characteristics. Although farmers had practiced selective breeding for centuries, the new scientific discoveries allowed faster and more accurate results. New varieties of crops such as corn, wheat, and rice were capable of producing far more grain than previously grown varieties. As a result of new animal breeding programs, developed nations were able to produce milk of higher quality and more meat.

Norman Borlaug developed high-yield crops, sparking the Green Revolution.

Farmers in developing countries fell behind in food production. This sparked the Green Revolution in the mid-twentieth century, a term that has come to describe the efforts by scientists in developed countries to engineer high-yield seeds for farmers in developing countries, especially in Asia and Latin America. The Green Revolution helped developing countries produce more food as the high-yielding grains became more widely available for sale there. Grain production in many countries more than doubled during the Green Revolution.[1] However, these crops often did not grow well in environments that were different from where they were developed. The modified crops also required more water, fertilizers, and pesticides than many farmers in developing nations had access to.

The spread of industrial agriculture throughout the world has provided countless people with vital nutrition. This system continues to efficiently produce food for billions of people. Many believe the industrial system of agriculture is the only system that can support such a large population of humans on Earth. Unfortunately, this model of agriculture has also led to a variety of serious problems. If we cannot find sustainable solutions to these problems, we risk depleting Earth's energy resources, polluting its waters, damaging its soils, and jeopardizing the health of current and future generations of people and wildlife.

NORMAN BORLAUG AND THE GREEN REVOLUTION

Agricultural scientist Norman Borlaug was a major contributor to the Green Revolution. In the mid-twentieth century, while researching in Mexico, he developed wheat varieties that produced exceptionally high yields. Due to Borlaug's work, wheat production in Mexico tripled. The high-yielding varieties of grain Borlaug developed helped many countries produce enough food to nourish their entire populations. Borlaug won the Nobel Peace Prize in 1970 for his contributions to agriculture.

THE IMPORTANCE OF SUSTAINABLE AGRICULTURE

Industrial agriculture allows people to harvest ever-increasing amounts of food and other products from the land. Yet, millions still go hungry. What if we could produce enough food to meet the needs of everyone on Earth without damaging the environment? This is what sustainable agriculture seeks to accomplish, and though difficult, this accomplishment is of the utmost importance. If we do not develop a sustainable system of agriculture, we risk a global crisis as more land becomes infertile and more human beings are born into hunger and poverty.

DEFORESTATION

When farmers in developing nations want access to more land for growing crops, they often cut down forests to create it. However, deforestation is one of the most harmful things humans do to the environment. It negatively impacts local plants and animals,

« **Slash-and-burn agriculture in the Amazon basin damages the environment.**

FOSSIL-FUELED AGRICULTURE

Industrial agriculture is highly dependent on fossil fuels. This nonrenewable form of energy is used to make and transport chemicals such as fertilizers and pesticides, apply the chemicals to the field, harvest and distribute products, process raw agricultural products, control the temperature of food, and much more. All in all, according to an FAO report on energy-smart agriculture, agriculture is responsible for approximately 30 percent of energy use worldwide.[2] In 2011, agriculture was approximately 6 percent of the world's economy.[3] Replacing nonrenewable energy with renewable energy harnessed from the sun, wind, water, or plants and ending other fossil fuel use will be necessary to meet agricultural needs without threatening the resources of future generations.

decreasing biodiversity. This is a particular concern in areas with tropical rainforests, which are the greatest centers of biodiversity in the world. Studies have shown deforestation is responsible for 17 percent of yearly human greenhouse gas emissions.[1]

Additionally, without tree roots to hold soil, fertile earth can be easily stripped away by wind or water. This process is called soil erosion. If there are chemicals in the soil, such as fertilizers or pesticides, they can contaminate nearby water sources if farmers are not taking precautions.

Sustainable technologies such as crop rotation and systems that raise livestock and crops together can keep a single area of land fertile for a long time, reducing the need for deforested land. Planting trees among crops or crops among trees can reduce deforestation while reaping the benefits of the fertile soil, moist shade, and biodiversity that trees provide.

FERTILIZERS

One of the most important current uses of chemicals on farms is to maintain fertile soil. Soil is one of the primary foundations of life on Earth, and it is a valuable natural resource. It is full of life, harboring billions of species of bacteria, fungi, insects, worms, and other organisms. Soil also gives life to growing plants. These plants in turn nourish both animals and people. In a natural cycle, the nutrients taken in by people and animals are returned to the soil, which fosters new life, and the cycle continues.

With manufactured chemical fertilizers, farmers do not need to recycle nutrients by returning them to the soil through manure or

TROPICAL RAINFORESTS

Today, approximately half of the tropical rainforests on Earth have been destroyed, and the remaining forests are rapidly being cut down in the name of agriculture.[4] The small percentage of land covered by tropical rainforests may contain up to 50 percent of wildlife species, many of them still undiscovered by humans.[5] Though we have yet to discover exactly how tropical rainforests came to be so rich in biodiversity, there is no question that the world's rainforests are priceless resources. New technologies and sustainable farming techniques, such as growing shade-loving coffee under a rainforest canopy, may be the key to saving what remains of these precious forests.

compost. They can just apply more chemical fertilizers. Each season, farmers need to apply more chemicals to get back to the same level of soil fertility. This cycle of removing nutrients from the soil is called soil mining. Although farmers in developed countries use better practices today, this is still an issue in parts of the world. As a result of this practice, soils around the world are gradually losing their fertility. Farmers can practice crop rotation to replenish nutrients in the soil. However, this system is imperfect: for example, corn and tobacco remove more nitrogen from the soil than other plants such as soybeans can put back.

The increasing amounts of fertilizers needed to grow crops are polluting Earth's water and disrupting natural ecosystems. When it rains, fertilizers are washed into rivers, lakes, and oceans, and they also filter down through the soil into the groundwater used for drinking.

SOIL BALANCE

In order for plants to grow well in soil, the soil needs to contain the right mix of chemicals for the plants. The primary chemicals plants need to grow are nitrogen, phosphorus, and potassium, which are elements found in nature. Farmers use fertilizers containing one or more of these chemicals to help their plants grow better and produce more food. But these fertilizers often do not contain the small amounts of other nutrients plants need, such as trace minerals like copper. Soils treated with incomplete mixes of fertilizers year after year will eventually become unproductive because the mix of chemicals in the soil becomes unbalanced.

Satellite photos show massive green algae blooms, such as this bloom in Lake Erie.

Fertilizers in lakes and oceans cause algae to bloom rapidly, throwing off the natural balance of the ecosystem in a process called eutrophication. The algae bloom blocks sunlight and uses up oxygen. This often results in large numbers of fish and other aquatic life dying. Too much fertilizer in groundwater can be dangerous as well, making the water toxic to drink.

POTENT PESTICIDES

Pesticides such as DDT that came into widespread use in the mid-twentieth century lowered costs to farmers and increased yields by up to 50 percent in some areas.[6] However, they also poisoned the environment, lodging in soils, contaminating water, and killing many plants and animals—including the natural predators of pests. Farm workers who sprayed the pesticides, people who drank contaminated food or water, and people who accidentally came into contact with the chemicals were at risk of pesticide poisoning. *Silent Spring*, a book by biologist and writer Rachel Carson, was instrumental in raising awareness of the dangers posed by the pesticides used at that time. In response to the concerns brought up in part by *Silent Spring*, DDT was banned in the United States in 1972.

Since fertilizer is so vital to the success of agriculture, people are exploring ways of using it more efficiently. New technologies for applying fertilizer can reduce the amount of fertilizer needed to nourish crops. Strategic placement of fertilizer and landscaping that prevents runoff can help stop water pollution. To maintain soil health, farmers must put nutrients back into it that are equal to what their crops took out. Adding compost is one method. Another additive that returns nutrients to the soil is biochar. Biochar is created when organic materials such as wood, manure, or leaves are heated without oxygen. Evidence suggests people in the Amazon and in Japan have been using biochar to improve their soil for thousands of years. Farmers have also rediscovered that raising livestock along with crops gives them a built-in source of natural fertilizer, saving them the cost of chemicals and recycling farm nutrients through animal waste.

PESTICIDES

Another problem with industrial agriculture is the use of pesticides. Insects, diseases, and weeds are considered pests because they can harm or destroy crops and livestock. For food production to be sustainable, farmers need to have ways of controlling pests. In industrial agriculture, pesticides—including insecticides, herbicides, and fungicides—are used for this purpose because they are usually effective and require little labor.

However, many pesticides are harmful to the environment. They are often toxic not only to the pests they are meant to control, but also to other plants and animals. The toxins in pesticides can spread, blown by wind or carried in water. Another problem with pesticides is that pests tend to develop a resistance to pesticides over time. Eventually, widely used pesticides no longer work. Scientists must then develop new pesticides, often more toxic than the ones previously used. For agriculture to be sustainable, we need a method of controlling pests without damaging the health of our planet. Sustainable methods of pest control attempt to encourage nature's defense mechanisms so the system maintains itself.

MONOCULTURE

Using chemical fertilizers and pesticides, many farmers grow only one crop over a large area, year after year. This practice is called monoculture. Farmers in a monoculture system only need the knowledge and equipment to manage one crop. It is a simple system, and thus it is more efficient for the farmer than a system with a lot of diversity. However, monoculture is also risky.

Since different crops use different nutrients, growing a single crop over a long period of time robs the soil of the nutrients that crop needs. Monoculture also encourages pests by providing them with a wide expanse of their favorite food and habitat year after year. These problems increase farmers' dependence on fertilizers and pesticides.

Monoculture also makes crops more vulnerable to pests and diseases. For example, say you were tending a garden where a lot of different crops were growing. You might notice that your tomatoes looked sickly and diseased, while all of your other crops were healthy. You could lose quite a few tomato plants and still have plenty of other crops to eat or sell. But if you had devoted your entire garden to tomato plants, you could have lost them all.

More and more, people in the agricultural community are noting the importance of biodiversity in the movement toward sustainable agriculture. Biodiversity makes farms more stable and less vulnerable to devastation from disease, climate change, and changes in consumer demand. It also helps naturally control pests and conserve resources, such as water and soil nutrients. Farmers can increase the biodiversity on their farms in many ways, including planting more varieties of crops, providing habitat for native wildlife, and raising both crops and livestock. However, adding crops or livestock increases farming costs for equipment, facilities, and labor. The farmer must also learn to manage multiple systems and processes.

CARBON DIOXIDE AND
CLIMATE CHANGE

Carbon is an element and a basic building block of life. Earth's carbon is constantly cycling, absorbed into vegetation, soil, and water, then emitted again into the atmosphere. Carbon attaches to oxygen to form the molecule carbon dioxide (CO_2).

Carbon dioxide is a greenhouse gas. That means it traps heat inside Earth's atmosphere. Increased levels of carbon dioxide and other gases in Earth's atmosphere have caused Earth to warm. Scientists agree the world's forests are some of the best weapons against climate change. Trees store large amounts of carbon in their trunks and roots, taking it out of the atmosphere in a process called carbon sequestration. In fact, forest ecosystems are capable of storing more than one trillion short tons (900 billion metric tons) of carbon. That is approximately double the amount of carbon dioxide currently floating in our atmosphere.[7] However, forests today are being destroyed so quickly that they are putting more carbon dioxide into the atmosphere than they are taking out.

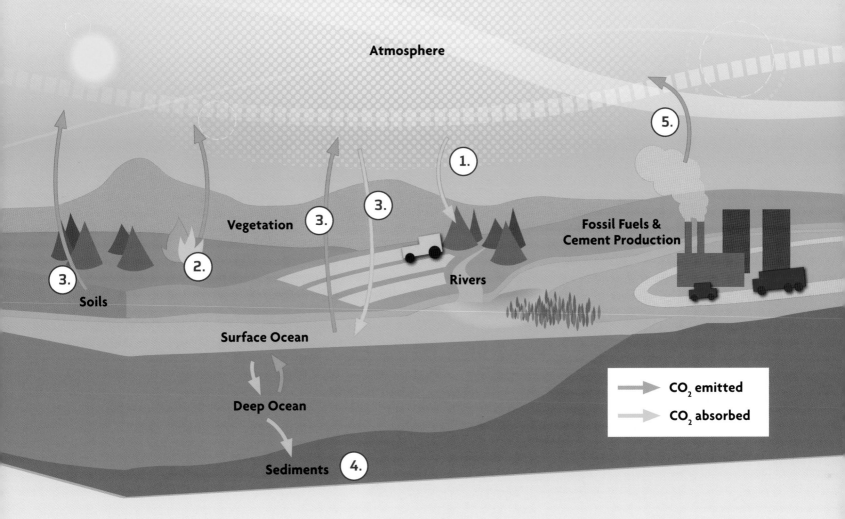

1. Plants absorb carbon dioxide in order to live.

2. When plants are burned, they release carbon into the air. When they decompose, their carbon goes into the soil.

3. Carbon also transfers between soil and air and between water and air.

4. The deep ocean and sediments below the ocean store large amounts of carbon.

5. The production of fossil fuels and products such as cement releases carbon that was stored in the soil millions of years ago.

CHAPTER 4

THE NEED FOR SUSTAINABLE ENERGY

Nearly every day in the news, you can hear buzzwords such as *fossil fuels*, *emissions*, and *energy crisis*. These words are trying to describe a global problem in the way we use energy. The problem is that approximately 80 percent of the energy we use comes from fossil fuels, such as gasoline, coal, and natural gas.[1] These limited energy resources formed inside Earth hundreds of millions of years ago. When we use them up, they will be gone forever. In addition to permanently draining Earth's natural resources, use of fossil fuels also pollutes our environment. The production and use of these fuels puts out harmful gases that create health problems and contribute to climate change.

Agriculture is a huge contributor to the problem of unsustainable energy use. Food production accounts for nearly one-third of energy use and one-fifth of greenhouse

Fossil fuels are used to power farm equipment.

gas emissions worldwide.[2] This energy use is out of proportion with agriculture's share of the world economy, which is only 6 percent.[3] As the price of fossil fuels rises, the cost of producing and transporting food also increases. Rising energy and food costs, growing awareness of the consequences of our dependence on fossil fuels, and fear of a looming energy shortage have driven scientists and farmers around the world to explore more sustainable options for energy.

Strategies for conserving energy—such as using more fuel-efficient machines and distributing products locally—can help our fossil fuel reserves last longer while saving both farmers and consumers money. Some farmers have taken the movement toward sustainable energy a step further by generating their own energy on the farm. Farmers are also responsible for producing a promising alternative to fossil fuels: biofuels.

WIELDING THE WIND

Between 2004 and 2007 alone, the world's use of wind power increased by more than 60 percent.[4] According to the wind power industry, approximately 12 percent of the world's electricity could be generated by the wind by 2020.[5] While substituting wind power for fossil fuels would have clear benefits for everyone, farmers might stand to gain the most from wielding the power of wind.

Ecologically friendly wind turbines can be used on farms.

Many of the windiest places are on flat, open farmland. Utility companies will pay farmers $2,000 or more per year in exchange for permission to install a wind turbine on their farmland.[6] If a farmer has a lot of space for wind turbines, this can be a great source of income for the farmer as well as a way to help the environment. Farmers can also install wind turbines for their own use. Wind turbines take up very little ground space. Farmers can continue to grow crops or let their livestock graze on the land beneath the turbine. Thus, the farmer's land becomes doubly valuable as a source of both energy and food.

WIND TURBINE SYNDROME

Some believe wind turbines cause major health problems in individuals who are sensitive to noise and vibrations. Symptoms of wind turbine syndrome include sleep deprivation, headaches, ringing or buzzing in the ears, dizziness, nausea, and anxiety. Some experts claim wind turbine syndrome can affect livestock as well as people. Some families and farmers have chosen to move away from wind farms due to the severity of the above symptoms. Many who argue that similar symptoms could easily be caused by something else have challenged Pierpont's research and noted that vibrations or noises from wind turbines may be annoying but are not a health risk.

Wind turbines are expensive, however, and it may take several years for them to pay for themselves. Wind power is limited by access to land and strong winds, and the huge turbines can be eyesores. Low quality or narrow roads make it difficult to transport the equipment to its desired location. Ill-placed wind turbines can confuse migrating birds or destroy important habitats for wildlife. The motion of the turbine's blades also changes the temperature of the air near the turbine. In some cases, this can be beneficial, with turbines cooling crops during the day, keeping them warm at night, and keeping them dry to prevent disease. On the other hand, wind turbines may dry out crops too much, requiring farmers to use more water. For most people, though, the benefits of wind farming greatly outweigh these negative effects.

STORING THE SUN

The sun has enormous potential as a source of renewable energy. Solar power could easily meet the energy needs of everyone on Earth now and in the future. However, even the most advanced technologies we have for collecting and converting solar energy are extremely inefficient—not to mention costly—and take up a lot of space.

Despite these challenges, many farmers are finding ways to use the sun's energy to make their operations more sustainable. According to a US Department of Agriculture (USDA) survey, solar panels are the most popular way of producing renewable energy on farms in the United States.[7] Even without expensive solar panels, farmers can use energy from the sun in many ways.

FOOD MILES

The concept of food miles is raising awareness of how far our food has to travel to reach us. In the United States, the produce you eat has been shipped an average of nearly 2,000 miles (3,220 km) before it reaches your plate.[8] The large amounts of fossil fuel energy required to transport food, and the harmful emissions produced in the process, generally make it less environmentally harmful to buy food from local sources. However, if local farming practices are not sustainable, this can sometimes cancel out the benefits of buying food locally.

A common application for solar energy on farms is heating greenhouses. After paying $700 in a single month to heat his greenhouse, New Mexico farmer Don Bustos decided to install solar collectors. These collectors gather the sun's energy, using it to heat water that is then pumped through tubes below the soil's surface to warm crops' roots. The soil insulates the water, keeping it from cooling down as it travels beneath the plants. The system saved Bustos $2,000 in energy costs the first year and increased his yields.[9] Solar collectors can be used to heat both air and liquids, such as water or antifreeze.

Steven Schwen, a Minnesota farmer, cleverly designed his greenhouse so windows face south, where the most sun will shine in. The north side is built into a hill, where the earth serves as natural insulation. The floor of the greenhouse is made with river rocks. It has water-filled tubes running under the floor that store the sun's heat over the course of the day and then release that heat at night. Finally, Schwen installed a solar-powered fan to keep the warm air close to the plants, where it is most needed. These technologies, called thermal banking, use the sun's energy to keep crops, livestock, and people warm while reducing energy costs and air pollution.

« **Greenhouses take advantage of the sun's energy.**

BIOFUEL BUMMERS

Although they are a step in the right direction, biofuels are not a perfect answer to sustainable agriculture and energy. A lot of land is needed to produce biofuels, and that land would take away from food production and wildlife habitat. Additionally, a switch to biofuels may not do enough to reduce greenhouse gas emissions. According to an analysis of biofuels in the journal *Science*, if the main goal of biofuels is stopping climate change,

> Policy-makers may be better advised in the short term (30 years or so) to focus on increasing the efficiency of fossil fuel use, to conserve the existing forests and savannahs, and to restore natural forest and grassland habitats on cropland that is not needed for food.[12]

Furthermore, as the demand for biofuels increases, the prices of biofuel crops such as corn may go up. This would make many foods more expensive, creating an unsustainable system.

LIQUID BIOFUELS

Farmers can actually produce renewable energy by growing certain crops or raising certain animals. Fuels made from plant or animal products or wastes are called biofuels, and they represent an innovation in sustainability that could potentially change how we use energy. According to former USDA undersecretary Gale Buchanan, "Bioenergy will be the biggest change in agriculture in our history."[10]

As of 2012, ethanol was the most widely used biofuel.[11] It is a liquid fuel made from starches and sugars. Corn and sugarcane are the most important crops for producing ethanol. As a liquid

This plant in Iowa produces ethanol.

fuel, ethanol can easily replace gasoline without much modification to vehicles and gas stations. The downside is that ethanol contains less energy than gasoline and can be difficult to produce.

Government subsidies have ensured the profitability of growing corn for ethanol production. However, ethanol produced from corn grown unsustainably will not solve the energy problem, and other crops may be better for producing ethanol. Crops with a lot of cellulose, or woody fiber, are being explored as alternatives. Farmers can grow these kinds of crops in a variety of conditions without the help of fertilizers, pesticides, or irrigation. Scientists and engineers have not yet come up with an efficient way to produce ethanol from cellulose, but cellulosic ethanol promises much higher energy and much lower emissions in comparison with ethanol from other crops.

Biodiesel, made from oils, is another common liquid biofuel. Biodiesel mixes with or replaces diesel made from fossil fuels. Farmers growing soybeans, canola, and other crops whose seeds contain a lot of oil have the ingredients to make biodiesel. In 2012, Europe was the world leader in using biodiesel.[13] As with ethanol, biodiesel is only as sustainable as its source.

Many farmers make their own biofuels and use them to power farm equipment. Dan West grows fruit trees in Missouri, and he makes fruit wines and ethanol from the wasted fruit each season. The ethanol costs him just 65 cents per gallon plus labor, and he uses it to fuel his tractor and mower.[14] Roger Rainville is trying to establish energy self-sufficiency on his farm in Vermont. He grows canola and processes the biodiesel himself. Since Rainville also raises dairy cows, he can use the waste from the seed processing as feed or sell it to local livestock farmers.

BIOGAS

Biogas is a type of biofuel that is made primarily by capturing methane gas from animal manure. The natural gas you likely use to heat your home and power your stove—a fossil fuel—is mostly methane, so biogas serves as an alternative. An added advantage of biogas is that capturing methane to use as energy keeps this potent greenhouse gas out of Earth's atmosphere.

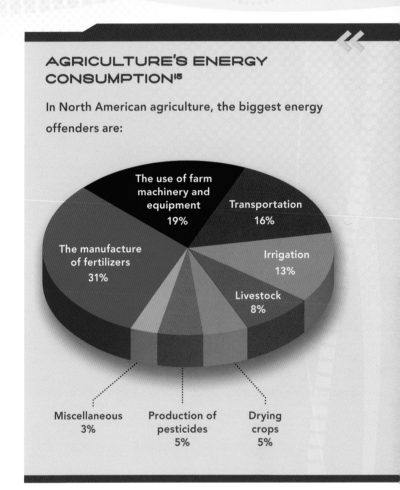

AGRICULTURE'S ENERGY CONSUMPTION[15]

In North American agriculture, the biggest energy offenders are:

- The use of farm machinery and equipment 19%
- Transportation 16%
- Irrigation 13%
- Livestock 8%
- Drying crops 5%
- Production of pesticides 5%
- Miscellaneous 3%
- The manufacture of fertilizers 31%

WHAT CAN YOU DO?

By changing how you eat, you can do a lot to help make agriculture more sustainable:

- Buying locally grown produce and locally raised meat and dairy products can help reduce consumption of fossil fuels in addition to supporting local farmers. You can even try growing your own food.
- Since it takes far more energy to raise meat than it does to grow vegetables, eating less meat is a good way to help agriculture become more sustainable.
- Stay away from processed foods. Processing requires energy, and processed foods are often less healthy for you.

To get from manure to methane, you need a digester. A digester is a system that uses bacteria to break down animal wastes, separating the gases from the solids and liquids. The process yields two valuable products. The biogas moves through a pipe to a location where it can be used or stored. The nutrient-rich solids and liquids left in the digester can be used as fertilizer, or they are sometimes added to animals' feed.

However, digesters are expensive, and they can be tricky to manage. Since it takes large amounts of manure to produce enough methane to use for fuel, this technology will mainly be useful for large-scale farms until people find ways to make the system more efficient. Storing the methane gas is another obstacle. Since methane cannot be condensed into liquid, huge amounts of space can be needed to store the unused gas.

FUELING THE FUTURE

Biofuels currently in the early stages of development include methanol, butanol, and dimethyl ether (DME). Methanol is an alcohol made from wood. It burns well and could potentially replace gasoline as a fuel. It is also cheaper to produce and use than ethanol. However, methanol only has half the energy content as the same amount of gasoline. It is also extremely poisonous, and drinking methanol can cause blindness or death. Butanol is a liquid fuel made from sugars, and it is much more similar to gasoline than ethanol is. High production costs stand in the way of widespread use. DME has the highest energy efficiency and lowest harmful emissions of any biofuel, but more research needs to be done to develop efficient, low-cost ways of producing and using the fuel.

As new technologies are developed to make alternative sources of energy available, you will have more choices about the types of energy and fuels you use. The adoption of biofuels will make sustainable agriculture even more important, as future farmers may be producing not only the world's food, but also its energy. Farmers who have diverse, resilient systems and who also grow, process, or generate their own energy may even be able to become completely self-sufficient, which is the peak of sustainability.

CHAPTER 5

BIOTECHNOLOGY AND GENETIC ENGINEERING

Over the past several decades, the amount of land that can be used for agriculture has steadily decreased. This is primarily due to soil degradation and the expansion of cities. At the same time, world population is rising. To compound the problem, people in wealthier parts of the world are eating more meat. To keep up with this demand, more land and energy is used for growing food for animals instead of food for humans. But this is not sustainable. Raising livestock requires much more land and energy than growing crops. One way to produce more food on less land is to develop types of plants and animals that yield more food per plant or animal.

BIOTECHNOLOGY

Biotechnology is a high-tech word for a practice that goes back to the beginnings of agriculture. It is the practice of using or changing living organisms to make useful

« **A local woman shows the high-yield rice grains which are being used to help her impoverished village in Vietnam.**

products. One of the earliest forms of biotechnology was selective breeding, or choosing the most desirable plants or animals to breed the next generation of crops or livestock. After thousands of years of this type of selection, we have many varieties of a given crop or animal suited to different people and places.

A practice called crossbreeding takes selective breeding to the next level. Selective breeding can only enhance traits already present in a type of plant or animal. Crossbreeding can combine traits from two different types within the same species. For example, a type of apple tree that produces very sweet fruit might be crossbred with another type of apple tree that produces very tart fruit. The hope would be that the hybrid, or offspring of the crossbred plants, would have a better balance of sweetness and tartness.

FOOD FOOTPRINTS

Raising livestock for meat requires more land and energy than growing food crops. The International Assessment of Agricultural Knowledge, Science and Technology for Development included the following statistics in its 2009 global report:

- Enough food was produced in 1993 to feed more than 100 percent of the world's population on a vegetarian diet. However, only 56 percent of the population could be sustained on a diet including 25 percent animal products.
- In the 1990s, approximately 40 percent of grain was grown as animal feed instead of human food. The percentage has likely increased with the growing demand for meat.
- It takes approximately 4.4 pounds (2 kg) of grain to produce 2.2 pounds (1 kg) of chicken, 8.8 pounds (4 kg) of grain to produce 2.2 pounds (1 kg) of pork, and 15.4 pounds (7 kg) of grain to produce 2.2 pounds (1 kg) of beef.[1]

    What can you do? Eat less meat and more vegetables. Not only is this a more sustainable way of eating, it is likely healthier as well.

Selective breeding and crossbreeding remain important agricultural technologies today. Since scientists now understand how genes are inherited, they can more accurately predict what will happen when selecting and crossbreeding to enhance certain traits.

HIGH-YIELDING VARIETIES AND NEW GOALS

During the twentieth century, plant breeders were primarily focused on developing high-yielding varieties (HYVs) of cereal grains—crops that produced more food. Cereal grains are the most widely grown and important food crops because they are nutritious, easy to store, and can be prepared in a variety of ways. HYVs have played an important role in reducing hunger in many developing countries. However, they have also come at a price.

GENETIC ENGINEERING 101

The process of creating a genetically modified organism is difficult in practice, but it is easy to understand once you know the basics. A trait corresponds to one—or perhaps a few—genes. The genetic material, or DNA, contained in each cell of a living organism is made up of countless genes. To transfer a gene from one organism into another organism, you must first isolate the gene you want to transfer. Once the gene is identified, special proteins called restriction enzymes are used to cut out the gene. Once this is done, the isolated gene is combined with a substance that will allow it to pass through another organism's natural defense mechanisms. Bacteria and viruses are often used for this. Once the new gene, or transgene, is established in an organism, the organism can pass the transgene on to its offspring.

ADVANCES IN LIVESTOCK BREEDING

The twentieth century has also seen significant advances in livestock breeding technologies, including artificial insemination (AI), embryo transfer (ET), and sexed semen. AI is the process of collecting a male animal's sperm and transferring the sperm into a female animal's uterus so it can fertilize an egg. This technology is primarily used in cattle and swine. It is also becoming more common for sheep and goats. It allows one high-quality male to have offspring with many females.

ET involves stimulating a female cow to produce multiple eggs at once. The fertilized eggs are transferred to develop inside other cows. ET greatly increases the number of calves a cow can have in her lifetime. However, the technology is still being refined. Livestock producers can use sexed semen in which the sperm has been sorted to increase their odds of getting offspring of the preferred sex.

Animal biotechnology has lagged behind plant biotechnology, especially in developing countries. Experts in the field are looking for ways to help farmers in developing countries improve their livestock by combining AI, ET, and other technologies. It is believed this will help reduce hunger and poverty in struggling communities. But as with plant biotechnology, animal biotechnology carries risks. New breeds or crossbred animals might not be as well adapted to a given environment as native breeds. They might also be more vulnerable to local diseases. These new breeds can also crowd out native breeds, reducing genetic diversity.

HYVs are usually adapted to the environments where they are developed. This means many HYVs are adapted to developed nations such as the United States. Because HYVs often struggle in foreign climates and have little resistance to local pests and diseases, they require large amounts of fertilizers and pesticides to produce their high yields. These chemicals can damage the environment. Additionally, many farmers in developing countries cannot afford to

« A farmer in Malawi waters his cornfield. Developing drought-resistant crops continues to be a challenge for researchers.

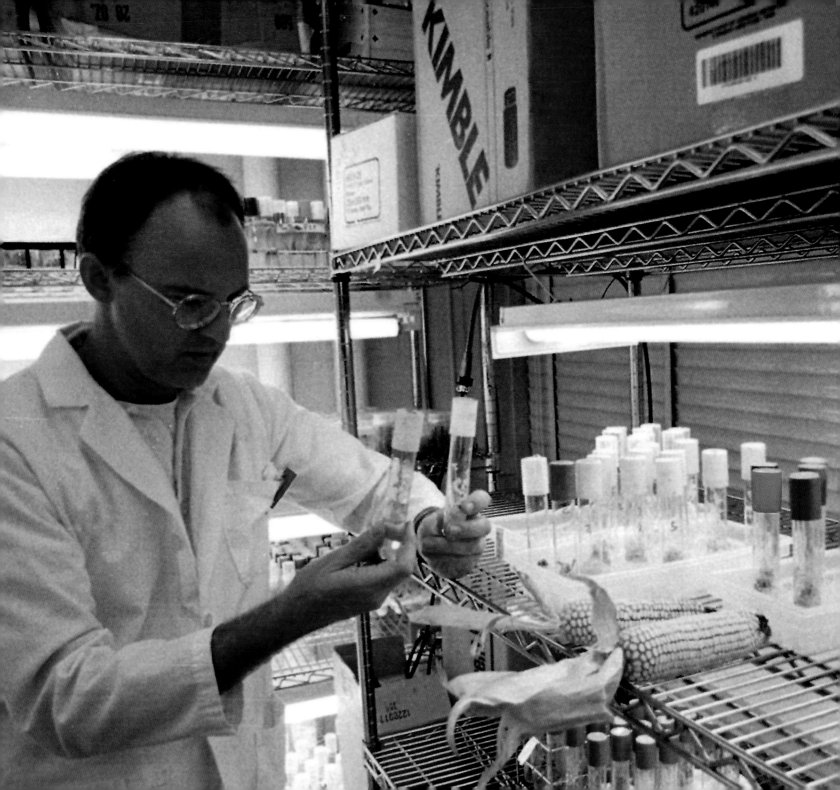

buy enough fertilizers and pesticides. These farmers often have less success with the HYVs than they did with traditional varieties. Furthermore, replacing traditional crops with ill-adapted HYVs reduces biodiversity and makes these crops more vulnerable to damage.

Scientists and plant breeders are developing new varieties of crops that will be more beneficial to farmers around the world. One way of doing this is involving farmers in the research and development of these varieties, a process called participatory research or participatory plant breeding. Participatory approaches take advantage of farmers' intimate knowledge of their crops, cultures, and environments. If a variety can be specifically tailored to the needs of a community, then both farmers and consumers will be more likely to accept the new variety. If that variety is also adapted to the local environment, it will flourish.

Researchers are also working to develop varieties that produce high yields even under poor conditions, such as extreme temperatures, too little or too much water, or a lack of nutrients. Some of these traits are more difficult to breed into plants than others. Drought tolerance—a plant's ability to grow well in dry, hot conditions—has proven to be a particular challenge. However, crops with these traits will become even more important in a future of unpredictable weather and declining soils.

« **A scientist conducts genetic research on corn.**

GENETIC ENGINEERING

In the late twentieth century, scientists found they could identify and cut out a specific gene from one organism and then transfer that gene to another organism. This technology, called recombinant DNA technology, is what genetic engineering (GE) most commonly refers to.

One of the main advantages of GE is that it allows breeders to take a desirable trait from one species and transplant it into a completely different species. In transferring specific, known genes instead of hoping for beneficial combinations of genes, GE also has more predictable and precise results than other breeding methods.

GENETICALLY MODIFIED CROPS

Plant breeding is the primary focus of GE in agriculture. The two main categories of genetically modified (GM) crops currently in use are insect-resistant crops and herbicide-tolerant crops. Most insect-resistant GM crops contain a

GE SUCCESS

A number of other GE experiments have also proven successful. A variety of GM papaya resistant to a devastating virus has saved papaya crops in Hawaii and other areas. Golden rice, a variety of GM rice that contains essential nutrient provitamin A, addresses chronic malnutrition in poverty-stricken areas. The addition of provitamin A in the diets of people who survive solely on rice might prove to prevent blindness caused by provitamin A deficiency.

gene from the bacterium *Bacillus thuringiensis* (Bt). This bacterium produces a toxin harmful to a narrow range of insects.

Since the crops themselves are resistant to harmful insects, there is no need to apply large amounts of insecticides to Bt crops. This reduces crop loss, costs to the farmer, damage to the environment, and harm to workers spraying insecticides. Additionally, since Bt toxin targets only a few specific insects, there is less risk that it will kill insects and other animals that are good for crops.

Bt cotton is the most common Bt crop. Studies conducted by biotechnology expert Clive James in 2004 and 2007 suggest that more than two-thirds of all cotton grown in China and more than 85 percent of all cotton grown in South Africa is Bt cotton.[2] Some studies have shown that Bt crops have significantly reduced the use of insecticides, whereas other studies suggest farmers of Bt crops have not changed their insecticide use.

Herbicide-tolerant crops allow farmers to spray herbicides more efficiently without the risk of harming their crops. More than 75 percent of GM crops grown worldwide are herbicide-tolerant crops.[3] The most common are soybeans, canola, corn, and cotton.

One pressing worry about insect-resistant and herbicide-tolerant crops is that their widespread, long-term use will cause insects to become resistant to Bt toxin and weeds to become resistant to herbicides used on GM crops. This would require new technologies to be developed, and in the meantime it would likely lead to increased use of insecticides and herbicides. Researchers are busy seeking answers to end this vicious circle.

Current and future goals for GE crop development include higher-yielding crops, crops that offer higher nutrition for undernourished communities, and crops that are resistant to more types of pests and diseases. Researchers are also studying plants that grow in harsh environments in the wild. By understanding the genetic makeup of these hardy plants, scientists hope to genetically engineer crops that will thrive even in poor soil, extreme temperatures, and areas struck by drought. Much progress has already been made toward these goals. The future

AQUADVANTAGE?

Salmon may be the first genetically engineered animal approved for human consumption. As of January 2012, the US Food and Drug Administration (FDA) was still in the process of evaluating the safety of AquAdvantage salmon. Biotechnology company AquaBounty Technologies has found a combination of genes that causes these salmon to grow twice as fast as non-GE Atlantic salmon. AquAdvantage salmon could allow farmers to raise more salmon with fewer resources in a shorter period of time. So far, the FDA has not found reason to believe these salmon would be unsafe to eat.

One concern about AquAdvantage salmon is that they could escape into the wild and compete with native salmon for food, space, and mates. If allowed to reproduce, the GE traits could spread to wild salmon. To address these fears, AquaBounty planned to sell only sterile salmon. In addition, they will make sure the GE salmon are contained with little risk of escaping. However, many worry the farmers raising these fish will not follow proper precautions. The FDA's decision will influence the global response to the human consumption of GE animals.

may even hold GM food crops that contain vaccines or medicines. This could be especially important in developing countries, where many lack access to health care.

GENETICALLY MODIFIED ANIMALS

GE technologies have been applied to livestock since the late twentieth century. The ability to genetically engineer animal growth hormones in mass quantities led to increases in the production of meat and dairy. Dairy cows injected with the synthetic hormone produce up to 30 percent more milk.[4] Livestock injected with the hormone grow faster and yield leaner cuts of meat. Though early tests seemed to show that meat and dairy from animals treated with growth hormone were safe, fear of unexpected negative effects is widespread. As a result, many countries have banned the use of growth hormones.

Other research in GE technology has been geared toward producing medicines and other substances in the milk, eggs, blood, and urine of livestock. This new application of GE has a lot of potential, but the risks are not thoroughly understood. In addition to fear and unknown risks, another major reason GE technology is not widely used on animals is poor reproductive rates. However, experts are currently working on ways to genetically engineer animals more successfully.

CONTAMINATED

CONTAMINATED

shaw's
Stop Genetically
Engineered Food

www.GREENPEACEusa.org

GE CONTROVERSY

Although genetic engineering has the potential to make agriculture sustainable by increasing food production, keeping down food costs, and contributing to human health and well-being, many believe it also has the potential for harm. They fear that tampering with nature in this way may have disastrous consequences.

One of the main concerns about GE is that it will cause the uncontrolled spread of modified genes. It is difficult to control where pollen and seeds from crops go. Instances of GM crops accidentally spreading have been reported, fueling worry among farmers and environmentalists alike. GM crops could mix with other varieties of crops and native species of plants. Due to patents and import bans, farmers can lose money if unwanted GM crops turn up in their fields. Spread of GM crops could encourage pests resistant to pesticides used in or on those crops. Furthermore, we do not yet know whether GM crops may have long-term effects on human health. These concerns have led the USDA to prevent GM crops from being certified as organic. Furthermore, scientists can react to existing problems—for example, by developing a crop's resistance to a new type of disease—by recombining genes they've found in nature. But this type of stop-gap approach is still inferior to the complex processes of nature, and will remain so unless technology greatly improves.

« Activists protested GE foods in Maine in 2002.

Another widespread concern is that GE technologies will benefit wealthy countries more than developing countries. Wealthy countries produce GM crops and distribute them to developing countries, presumably with good intentions. However, many GM crops are patented by large corporations. This means the corporations have control over and profit from the GM crops they develop, wherever they are grown. Many fear that wealthy countries and large corporations will eventually control—and even own—crops grown throughout the world.

PATENTS ON LIFE

If a person or a company has a patent on a product, that means no one else can make, use, or sell that product. In the late twentieth century, people were creating new varieties of crops through GE. They wanted to patent their products. However, many others believed they had no right to patent a living organism. Such patents would mean farmers could not save and replant seeds, as they had always done, without paying whoever had patented them. It would also give the patent holder control over the patented organism or gene wherever it happened to spread in the world. Allowing patents on living organisms continues to be a source of extreme controversy.

Other fears stem from speculation about GE humans, GE biological weapons, dangerous allergens, and developing resistance to antibiotics used in GE. The potential risks of GE have caused many countries to ban genetically modified organisms (GMOs). In countries that allow GE, the public has pushed for labeling of GM products so people can choose not to buy these products.

Proponents of GE believe panic about GE stems from misunderstanding. They say GE is really not much different from other breeding practices; it simply saves time. Crops and livestock that are not genetically engineered can pose many of the same threats as GE crops. Whether or not GE is a safe technology, it has such potential for improving agriculture that research will certainly continue. Time will tell whether GE and other biotechnologies will contribute to or detract from sustainable agriculture in the long run.

PRECISION AGRICULTURE

Precision agriculture technologies allow farmers to apply small amounts of fertilizers, pesticides, water, and other materials precisely where and when needed. Taking advantage of advances in computing power, Global Positioning Systems (GPS), and sensors, these technologies offer customized care for crops, reduce labor, improve yields, reduce the need for expensive and environmentally harmful chemicals, conserve water and energy resources, and provide many other benefits. Though still in various stages of development, these technologies are already acting as a bridge between current practices and a sustainable agriculture system, and they have promising futures.

 Farmers can use GPS devices to make their work more efficient.

PRECISION PESTICIDES

New equipment that gives farmers more control over pesticide application is helping reduce pesticide use and exposure. Special nozzles for sprayers can deliver less pesticide with better coverage. They can also help prevent the pesticide from drifting in the wind to an unwanted area. One type of nozzle that surrounds the spray of pesticide with a spray of water can reduce pesticide use by up to 50 percent.[1] Other types of nozzles spray very tiny droplets that cover crops well with a small amount of pesticide. Some nozzles even give the droplets a static charge so they will cling to plant leaves. After each spray with any of these nozzles, precise shutoff valves prevent extra chemicals from leaking onto the field.

FERTILIZER MICRODOSING AND PRECISION APPLICATION

Microdosing is a technique for applying low doses of fertilizer only where needed. This technique can be used on a small or large scale, using a low-tech or high-tech system. In microdosing, small amounts of fertilizer are applied to each individual plant during or after planting. This system has been particularly helpful in increasing crop yields in parts of Africa, where soils have lost fertility, drought is common, and farmers often cannot afford or do not have access to mass-produced fertilizers. Providing African farmers with fertilizers also helps prevent the common practice of abandoning infertile land and burning down forests to create more farmland.

However, the process of measuring out fertilizer and placing it in each hole along with the seeds can be a lot of work. To help farmers easily apply the correct amount of fertilizer for each plant, researchers are developing single-dose fertilizer tablets with premeasured amounts of fertilizer. Seeds coated with fertilizer may eventually replace tablet fertilizers as a way of increasing yields without also increasing labor, sparing farmers the need to apply a separate fertilizer tablet.

Banded fertilizer placement also reduces the amount of fertilizer needed. With this technique, fertilizer is applied in narrow bands close to the rows of crops, either on or below the surface of the soil. It reduces the amount of money farmers spend on fertilizers and the hazard to the environment. Additionally, precision application of fertilizer helps farmers avoid accidentally fertilizing weeds and helps minimize runoff of unused fertilizer.

NANOTECHNOLOGY

Nanotechnology, the science of creating microscopic devices, may be used to make farm management even more precise. Scientists are continually finding new ways to use nanotechnology in agriculture. Microscopic sensors could detect nutrients, water, or pollutants in soil. Materials with microscopic pores could filter harmful chemicals or make sure the correct doses are applied. Nanomaterials could even rid water and air of pollutants or provide clean energy. Researchers are exploring ways of using nanotechnology to help make agriculture sustainable.

«

Microirrigation helps conserve water in arid regions.

MICROIRRIGATION

Conserving water is very important for the sustainability of agriculture. Huge amounts of precious freshwater are used to irrigate crops worldwide. Entire landscapes and ecosystems have been changed or destroyed to divert water onto farmland. Formerly vast underground reservoirs are being depleted much more quickly than they refill. Though irrigation is often necessary, careless use of water has caused useable freshwater to become scarce in many parts of the world.

Microirrigation is a compelling solution to this problem. This technology uses less water by dripping, trickling, or spraying small amounts of water close to crops' roots. Pipes that release small, constant amounts of water are installed throughout the field. A control station allows farmers to manually or automatically control the amount of water used, the pressure used, and other factors. The ultimate goal is to apply water at the same rate as the plants absorb it.

By irrigating crop roots directly, farmers avoid watering weeds. In addition, many diseases thrive in moist conditions and tend to spread to plants with wet leaves. Microirrigation waters only the roots of plants, so leaves are left dry. Farmers can also use microirrigation systems to apply precise amounts of fertilizers and other chemicals by dissolving them in the water. Farmers can distribute water evenly without it running off hills or pooling in valleys. Furthermore, farmers do not need to stop work on their farm during microirrigation, as soil remains dry enough to support heavy farm equipment.

Users of microirrigation do face some challenges. Because the openings in the irrigation systems are so small, they are easily clogged and require a lot of maintenance to keep clear. Microirrigation systems can also be expensive to purchase and install, and they are easily

REMOTE SENSING

Remote sensing is a valuable technology for monitoring agricultural activity and creating maps for VRT. Sensors on satellites or airplanes produce images that help track deforestation, the spread of disease, nutrient deficiencies, and other important factors from high above the earth. Different wavelengths of light reflected on the sensors can show different types of insects, plants, and diseases. These images can be used to create maps so farmers can see areas with pest problems and take measures to control the pests or prevent their spread.

damaged. Small animals and insects can chew through the water lines, and people can break parts of the system by accidentally stepping on them or driving farm equipment over them. Still, the benefits of microirrigation systems outweigh the costs for some farmers.

VARIABLE RATE TECHNOLOGY

One of the most exciting new developments in sustainable agriculture is variable rate technology (VRT). Within each farm, different areas have different needs. Some areas of a farm might have fewer nutrients in the soil than others. Pests might be more of a problem in some areas than in others. And some areas might have enough water while other areas are dry. Farmers today generally apply the same amounts of fertilizers, pesticides, and water over their entire farm. Until recently, precision agriculture techniques have been too labor intensive for many farmers to want to use. VRT uses

»

Farm sensors such
as this one make
sophisticated VRT
systems possible.

computer-controlled systems, automated machines, and other technologies to apply customized amounts of many different materials to farmers' fields.

VRT is a complex system of different technologies that work together to help farmers precisely manage their soil. The first step in VRT is to gather information about the farm by taking soil and crop samples from different areas of the farm. These samples can be analyzed for moisture content, nutrients, pests, and other qualities. Researchers are also developing technologies that will take continuous samples so farmers will always have current information. Computers store and analyze all of this data using a geographic information system (GIS). Then the data is used to create customized recommendations for improving different areas of the farm.

In map-based VRT, GIS works in tandem with GPS images to produce detailed maps of the farm. These maps show farmers how water, nutrients, pests, or other factors are distributed in their fields. The maps can show the recommended amounts of materials, such as fertilizers or pesticides, to be applied to the soil. These maps tell computerized farm equipment where and how much to apply, and GPS keeps the machines on track.

Sensor-based VRT systems are newer than map-based systems. In these systems, the machines used to apply fertilizers, pesticides, or water are equipped with sensors. Different sensors can detect different things. Sensors on machines used to apply pesticides can detect insects or weeds and then immediately spray them. Some can sense the shapes and sizes of crops and adjust their spraying accordingly. Sensors on machines used to apply fertilizers can detect different nutrients in the soil and apply custom amounts or combinations of fertilizer. Similarly, sensors on machines used to irrigate fields can adjust the amount of water sprayed based on the amount of moisture already in the soil. The simultaneous testing and application of sensor-based

PRECISION FISHING

Fishing is one of the least sustainable branches of agriculture. Many current fishing practices, such as bottom trawling with a net dragged along the seafloor, tend to trap large amounts of fish and sea life other than the desired species. These unlucky sea creatures are called bycatch, and some of them, such as sea turtles, are now in danger of extinction. National Oceanic and Atmospheric Administration Teacher at Sea Heather Haberman says, "At times bycatch can make up as much as 90 percent of a fisherman's harvest."[2] Engineers have designed bycatch reduction devices (BRDs) and turtle excluder devices (TEDs) to help unwanted species escape from fishing nets. BRDs on shrimp nets are holes in the top of the net that fish can swim out of. Since shrimp are not strong swimmers, they cannot get out through the holes. TEDs are a set of bars near the opening of a net. The bars stop turtles and other large animals from entering the net but allow small animals to pass through.

VRT systems makes these systems more efficient than map-based systems. Sensor-based systems are becoming more common and will likely come into widespread use in the future.

The main problem with VRT is that it is expensive. For farms that have little variation in soil properties, moisture, or elevation, VRT would not be worth the investment. Additionally, VRT cannot predict or control the weather and other variables that affect crops. University of Manitoba soil scientist Don Flaten says,

> If you have precise geographical information but don't have a hot clue whether you're going to have a wet year or a dry year, it's like you're measuring one part of your crop-management system with a micrometer and then chopping it off with an axe.[3]

In many respects, farmers' knowledge and experience is still the best farm management tool. However, computer simulations let farmers and experts make more and more accurate predictions and forecasts that could help make VRT more effective. As computing power grows and our predictions become more accurate, VRT will continue to develop and become more effective, perhaps enough so to be widely used on farms. The conservation of resources allowed by VRT is one of farmers' many tools to improve sustainability.

Will Allen, founder of Growing Power, has harnessed the power of sustainable agriculture to grow healthy, affordable food right in the heart of the city. Allen produces mountains of fresh produce, meat, fish, dairy, and honey near a low-income area of Milwaukee, Wisconsin. Nearly 20,000 plants, more than 50 bins of worms, 14 beehives, thousands of fish, and livestock including chickens, ducks, rabbits, and goats thrive on Allen's farm headquarters.[4]

He makes his products easily accessible to his fellow city dwellers, who might otherwise be dependent on processed food or on food shipped from far away. People of all ages—especially children—visit the farm to learn more about sustainable agriculture. Allen does all this on just two acres (0.8 ha) of land, which is approximately the size of a soccer field.

In order to maximize the growing power of his small plot of land, Allen grows crops in greenhouses and in plastic garden shelters so he can produce food year-round. He stacks beds vertically and hangs pots to utilize every bit of space. The farm is on the cutting edge in trying out new ideas in sustainable agriculture and energy use. He also uses innovative technologies such as vermiculture and aquaponics instead of fossil fuel–derived fertilizers to make his soil fertile enough to produce large amounts of food.

Some 5,000 pounds (2,270 kg) of worms raised on Allen's farm can convert thousands of pounds of food waste into organic fertilizer in just a few months.[5] The worms feast on the waste,

Will Allen of Milwaukee's Growing Power

and what comes out the other end is full of nutrients. In Allen's aquaponics system, he raises local breeds of fish that had been decimated by overfishing. The nutrient-rich fish waste helps the plants grow, and the fish are also a valuable and profitable source of food. Water from the fish tanks, which is full of fish waste, flows into a bed of gravel and plants that break down nutrients and filter out solids. Then the water is used to fertilize crops and feed worms. The water can be reused again in the fish tanks.

Allen has received several awards for his work in sustainable agriculture, including a $500,000 "Genius Grant" from the MacArthur Foundation. But he isn't doing this for the awards. He is doing it in the hopes of building a healthier, more sustainable future.

CHAPTER 7

BIODIVERSE FARMING SYSTEMS

The more complex a community of life is, the more stable it becomes. Different species of plants and animals give each other checks and balances, preventing any one species from tipping the scales too steeply.

Over the past century or so, we have experienced the successes and failures of humankind's manipulation of nature to make it specific to our needs and to make it simpler and more efficient with industrial agriculture. As it became clear through damage to the environment that we were tipping the scales too steeply in our favor, people began looking to nature for a better solution.

Nature seems to sustain itself effortlessly. Even if we damage or alter it, nature is always finding ways to smooth out our ripples. What if we could grow crops without throwing nature out of balance? Biodiverse farming systems have the potential to do

« **Natural ecosystems are home to thousands of interacting species.**

just that. By studying how our environment naturally maintains fertility and controls pests, we can use the same techniques to our advantage without doing harm. The more self-renewing and self-sustaining our systems are, the closer we move toward being sustainable.

INTEGRATED PEST MANAGEMENT

The development of integrated pest management (IPM) has been a huge step in the direction of sustainable agriculture. According to the IAASTD Global Report, IPM can reduce pesticide use by up to 99 percent in some cases.[1] Created in response to environmental damage from chemical pesticides, IPM combines a variety of more eco-friendly, diverse approaches to pest control.

James Kendrick Jr., who was vice president for agriculture and natural resources at the University of California, said IPM "is based on an understanding of the entire ecological system to which the host that we are interested in keeping healthy belongs."[2] This way of managing pests requires extensive knowledge of all parts of an agricultural system, such as plants, animals, humans, soil, water, and chemicals. IPM experts provide farmers with pest-control strategies that will work with their system. The five major strategies are biological, genetic, chemical, cultural, and regulatory. IPM programs usually combine several different pest-control strategies.

Biological control encourages pests' natural predators. For example, if insects were eating the flowers in your garden, you might install a bird feeder nearby to attract birds to eat those insects. Genetic control uses GM plants or animals that are resistant to the pests. Chemical pesticides can be used for chemical control, though their use is kept to a minimum. Changes in the way farms are managed, such as rotating crops or planting at a different time, are methods of cultural control. Finally, regulatory control involves making laws or rules about pest management, such as forbidding certain pests or plants to be moved from one place to another.

INSECT CONTROL

Insects destroy up to 25 percent of the world's food crops every year.[3] This poses a hazard to the global supply of food. Encouraging predators that will eat or kill pest insects is an effective, sustainable way to control this threat. Farmers can attract helpful predators to their farms by providing them with food and habitat.

In general, the more kinds of plants and animals present on a farm—that is, the more biodiversity the farm has—the more likely the farm is to be home to natural predators of pests. Many farmers grow different kinds of plants with or around their crops to attract natural predators or parasites that will kill damaging insects. In recent decades, scientists have also developed insecticides that do not harm predators or parasites of pest insects. Thus, even if some insecticides are used, biological controls are still in place.

Crop rotation helps control insects by taking away that insect's favorite crop after just one growing season. This way, the population of one type of insect will not increase from season to season. Another strategy to deter insects is to grow plants that naturally repel them. For example, onions and carrots are commonly planted together because onions are thought to repel carrot flies, and carrots are thought to repel onion flies.

Taking an opposite approach, farmers can also grow plants that are even more attractive to pests than the main crop. When planted around the outside of the crop, these tempting plants lure insects away from the crop. This technique is called perimeter trap cropping. If necessary, insecticides can then be used on just the perimeter plants instead of on the entire crop. Research conducted by expert horticulturalist Jude Boucher shows the benefits of perimeter trap cropping:

In 2004, nine New England growers participating in Boucher's research used perimeter trap cropping to, on average, increase yields of cucumbers and other vine crops by 18 percent and reduce insecticide use by 96 percent. This led to an average increase in earnings of $11,000 per grower.[4]

WEED CONTROL

Integrated weed management (IWM), a form of IPM, is still developing as a sustainable approach to controlling weeds. It has not yet significantly

CONTROLLING DISEASE THROUGH BIODIVERSITY

Researchers have found that certain species of fungi, bacteria, and other microorganisms can control diseases. By encouraging these fungi and bacteria to grow or by adding them to plants or soils, farmers can control diseases biologically and reduce their use of pesticides. However, farmers must take care when introducing new species, as they can create new problems in an ecosystem even if they solve the original problem.

reduced the use of herbicides, but many farmers have found IWM to be effective. Rotating crops from season to season disrupts the cycles of persistent weeds and helps control them.

Farmers also need a sustainable way of preventing bare soil from being taken over by weeds between plantings. After a food crop is harvested, farmers can plant the bare land with a cover crop. Cover crops do not always produce food or income. They increase the farmer's seed, fuel, and labor costs to plant and remove. However, they suppress weeds, prevent soil erosion, and enrich the soil for the next crop. Cover crops can also attract pest predators, helping to stabilize the farm by increasing biodiversity.

Parasitic weeds that suck the life out of crops are a serious problem in many countries. In Africa, a parasitic weed called *Striga* is responsible for the loss of up to 80 percent of corn crops.[5] Plant breeders are working to

TYPES OF COVER CROPS

Different types of cover crops can be planted to focus on different problems. For example, legumes are often planted as cover crops because they add nitrogen, an important nutrient, to the soil. The nitrogen will help the next crop planted in that soil flourish. However, legumes are less effective at controlling weeds because the nitrogen also nourishes unwanted plants. Cover crops grown primarily to increase soil fertility are also called green manure. Grasses such as rye are better at suppressing weeds, but not as good for enriching the soil.

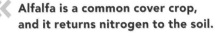

Alfalfa is a common cover crop, and it returns nitrogen to the soil.

develop varieties of crops—especially corn—that are resistant to *Striga* and other parasitic weeds through biotechnology and GE.

Researchers have found that certain plants are naturally harmful to weeds like *Striga*. In a phenomenon called allelopathy, these plants release chemicals that interfere with the growth of the weed. Growing such plants between rows of food crops, a practice called intercropping, is a natural way of suppressing the weeds. Allelopathy is still a bit of a mystery, but researchers are working on ways to put its advantages to greater use in sustainable agriculture.

DESTROYING STRIGA

Researchers have discovered that the plant *Desmodium* interferes with the life cycle of *Striga*. This plant is intercropped with corn to prevent *Striga* from damaging crops. However, intercropping would be much more useful if the crop used to stop *Striga* were also a food crop. Studying how *Desmodium* controls *Striga* may give researchers the information they need to breed plants that prevent the parasitic weed and also produce valuable food.

AGROFORESTRY

Today, many farmers wage war on trees, clearing them for farmland. This rapid deforestation decreases biodiversity and contributes to climate change. Agroforestry has the potential to reverse these effects while providing a wide variety of benefits to farmers, crops, and livestock.

Tea plants grow under a tree canopy in India.

A MIRACLE TREE

The tree *Faidherbia albida* is widely used in Africa for agroforestry. This tree is unique in that it sheds its leaves during the rainy season and leafs out in the dry season—the opposite of most other trees. This special characteristic makes it useful to farmers because it does not shade or compete with crops grown during the rainy season. During the dry season, the tree provides much-needed shade. It is also a legume, so it adds nitrogen to the soil, improving soil fertility. Additionally, the tree's leaves and seed pods are valued sources of food for livestock in the dry season, when other food is scarce.

The widespread adoption of agroforestry still lies in the future, but it has great potential to improve our environment, reverse climate change, and benefit both farmers and consumers.

Rows of trees planted along field edges provide protective barriers, preventing soil erosion from water or wind and stopping pollution from runoff. Strips of trees also serve as highways for beneficial wildlife that can help to pollinate plants or control pests. Trees grown within the borders of fields and pastures are also beneficial. Alley cropping is the practice of alternating rows of trees with rows of crops. This practice provides the same benefits of increased biodiversity and protection against erosion while also providing farmers with valuable crops such as nuts, fruits, and wood. Some crops and pasture grasses also grow better when partially shaded by trees.

Silvopasture is the similar practice of planting trees in a pasture used for grazing livestock. The trees used in silvopasture are valuable crops that also keep livestock healthier by shading them from the scorching sun. Another application of agroforestry is forest farming, or growing specialty crops that do well under the shade of a forest canopy. Some examples of good forest farm crops are medicinal herbs, mushrooms, coffee, cocoa, tea, and decorative ferns. These crops can be grown in forests of trees that produce wood, fruits, or nuts, or can be tapped for syrup. Forest farmers must choose crops carefully, planting new crops as trees grow and light conditions change.

CROP-LIVESTOCK SYSTEMS

Some farmers choose to raise both crops and livestock on the same farm. The complexity of crop-livestock systems means they require more knowledge and labor to maintain, but they can also be much more stable and profitable.

Crop-livestock systems create a closed system in which resources are recycled rather than having to be brought onto the farm from elsewhere. Parts of crops that are not meant for human use feed livestock. In turn, the manure and urine from livestock fertilizes the crops, which feed the livestock, which fertilize the crops, and so on. Because the nutrients are recycled, farmers have little or no need to buy expensive feeds and fertilizers.

In addition to providing convenient nutrient recycling, livestock animals are becoming increasingly valuable with the growing demand for meat. When families have extra income, they might buy a livestock animal, which they can sell or trade in times of need. Livestock animals are especially valuable to farmers who live in harsh climates where few crops can grow.

Other services animals provide for plants include tilling, weeding, and pest control. For example, rooting pig noses and roaming cattle hooves can improve the texture of the soil. Some farmers use these animals to break up the soil in preparation for planting seeds. Animals such as cattle, sheep, and goats will naturally control weeds when left to graze under tree crops or between rows of other crops they cannot eat. Chickens eat insects that would otherwise damage crops. Crop-livestock systems that have multiple kinds of crops and multiple kinds of

ANIMAL POWER

A main benefit of livestock animals in developing nations is their ability to provide farm labor. They can pull or carry heavy loads, aiding in work on the farm or transporting farm products to market. In addition to pulling their own weight on the farm, livestock can provide manure, an important source of energy for people. Dried manure can be used instead of wood to provide heat and light. Gases such as methane can also be extracted from animal manure and converted into energy people can use. Using biogas has the added benefit of keeping greenhouse gases out of Earth's atmosphere.

Oxen provide manure and muscle for farms in developing nations.

Fish thrive in the irrigation ditches between rice paddies.

animals tend to be more stable, minimizing risk to farmers if one type of plant or animal falls to disease, pests, or bad weather.

Fish can be an important addition to crop-livestock systems. For centuries, farmers in Asia have been using a sustainable crop-livestock-fish system in which crop wastes feed the livestock, livestock wastes feed the fish, and fish wastes feed the crops. Fish flourish in flooded rice fields, feeding on weeds and insects, while their wastes fertilize the rice. The success of Asian farmers has inspired farmers around the world to use new technologies, such as aquaponics, to further refine this centuries-old practice. Introducing fish into agricultural systems may also help lessen the impact of overfishing on the world's oceans and lakes. According to Paul Kiepe, a representative for the Africa Rice Center, "As fish catches are becoming smaller, [fish-crop systems] will be increasingly important for ensuring that food production provides people with enough protein."[6]

Though the benefits of biodiverse farming systems have been recognized since long ago, we are only now beginning to understand the intricacies of such complex systems. As these systems change, we will need to continually reevaluate our approach to sustainable agriculture, with the goal always being to move toward balance. Though balanced, biodiverse systems may require more knowledge, more labor, and more money at the outset. Farmers and scientists will continue to research, innovate, refine, adjust, and bring new technology to these systems to make them more sustainable.

PERENNIAL POWER

A future sustainable agriculture system will likely consist of mostly perennial plants. One perennial system used frequently today is the grass pastures on which animals graze. The plants return each year with no need to reseed. Not replanting every year minimizes soil damage and soil erosion. Perennials grow deep roots, making them less susceptible to drought and weather damage.

Perennials can form the basis of a self-sustaining system that is more similar to plants growing in nature. The most exciting research in perennial crops is investigating perennial grains. A field of perennial grains could be harvested repeatedly without replanting and disrupting the field's ecosystem.

CHAPTER 8

THE FUTURE OF SUSTAINABLE AGRICULTURE

The future of sustainable agriculture is precarious, but also promising. It depends on farmers and consumers, workers and policymakers, researchers and corporations all working together to meet the goals of environmental health, community support, and profitability. It depends on developing new technologies and practices that will increase both the efficiency and the resilience of farms. It also depends on getting the word out about these technologies and practices so more farmers and consumers can choose to support sustainable agriculture in effective ways.

Different people have different ideas of what sustainable agriculture should look like. Some envision a future of food genetically engineered to produce high yields, reduce the need for pesticides and herbicides, and provide added nutrition or life-saving medicines for the poor and malnourished people of the world. This vision

◀◀ **A farm adviser, *right*, teaches a farmer about sustainable practices.**

might include advanced pesticides that harm only a single type of pest or weed and machines that apply fertilizers, water, and pesticides so precisely that no material is wasted. This vision would require sustainable substitutes in place of fossil fuels. Others foresee a future in which all food is grown with biological controls instead of synthetic chemicals or genetic engineering. This view might include farms where biodiverse crops and livestock form a closed system that can easily adapt to changes in weather, pests, and diseases. Still others envision a combination of biological controls, genetic engineering, new chemicals and machinery, and new sources of energy when they think of sustainable agriculture in the future.

ORGANIC FARMING OR SECOND GREEN REVOLUTION?

In response to the need for more sustainable agricultural practices, organic farming is becoming more common. Organic crops and

---

WASTE NOT

Part of the problem of world hunger is that we waste so much food. Approximately one-third of the food produced worldwide goes to waste.[1] How often does your family throw out food you did not get around to eating? By planning your meals a bit more carefully, you can avoid buying too much food. There are also many ways to use food you would normally throw away. Vegetable scraps and meat bones can be used to make broth for soup. Mushy fruit can be blended into smoothies. Stale bread makes good bread crumbs or French toast. Additionally, most food scraps can be composted and later used to fertilize a garden.

livestock are grown or raised without the use of toxic pesticides, synthetic hormones, antibiotics, or GE.

The organic farming movement began in the 1930s, picking up speed over the next several decades. In the late twentieth and early twenty-first centuries, many of the world's countries settled on standards and guidelines for organic farming. Though these standards forbid the use of toxic chemicals and GMOs for the most part, organic farming today is far from old-fashioned. Advanced sensor technologies that monitor weather patterns and moisture, computerized systems that control irrigation, scientific analysis of nutrients and microorganisms in soil, and many other advanced technologies help organic farmers.

The market for organic food is rapidly increasing worldwide, particularly in the United States. Consumers of organic food feel safer knowing their food does not contain potentially harmful man-made substances. The increase in demand for organic food has led to an increase in organic farming. Organic farmers save money by not buying expensive chemicals and equipment, and they can generally sell their produce at a higher price. The health of the environment and of workers on organic farms also benefit from the lack of chemicals. An increase in organic farming seems likely in the future, as it has proven both environmentally

VERTICAL FARMING

Vertical farming may be the solution to meeting local and global food needs with little space. Skyscrapers built in the future by stacking gardens or greenhouses could help bring fresh food to cities, where populations will grow faster than anywhere else. These buildings would theoretically create space to grow food year-round, lower the cost of transporting food, and reduce the need for pesticides, fertilizers, and water.

However, the cost of constructing a vertical farm and the energy needed to create ideal conditions for crops—particularly lighting—pose significant challenges. Experts say rooftop farming or adding greenhouses to existing buildings may be a more practical solution.

friendly and profitable. However, current organic farming has its own problems, and it is not a silver-bullet sustainability solution.

Without the use of chemical pesticides, it is often more difficult to control pests. Without the use of chemical fertilizers and growth hormones, organic farmers generally cannot produce as much food as industrial farmers. Organic farming requires more knowledge than industrial farming, and organic certification is costly. It is often more labor intensive, too. Organic produce is often more expensive on supermarket shelves. This means it can be difficult for lower-income consumers to afford. Some argue that if all farmers adopted organic methods, world hunger would increase. However, the full price of industrial agriculture is not represented in

Current organic farming practices are a step down the path toward sustainability, but they are not the full solution.

its sticker price in the supermarket. The supermarket price does not include damage to the environment or harm to people's health.

Still, even firm supporters of industrial agriculture recognize that they cannot stay in business if they do not start moving toward what organic farming represents—sustainability. Industrial farmers can see the benefits of improving soil health, reducing pesticide and fertilizer use, and increasing biodiversity on their farms. This movement of mainstream agriculture toward sustainability has been called the second Green Revolution. Though the second Green Revolution still relies on chemicals and GM crops, it shows that organic farmers and industrial farmers share some of the same goals.

GROWING SMALLER AND CLOSER TO HOME

One of the biggest threats to sustainable agriculture is the corporatization of agriculture. Large agricultural corporations drive down prices and make it difficult for family-owned farms to stay in business. Today, many farmers stay in business by making contracts with large corporations. The farmer agrees to produce food for an agribusiness company in exchange for guaranteed profits. Often, the company will also supply the contract farmer with fertilizers, pesticides, and water. In this way, farmers become dependent on agribusiness companies whose survival may depend on the continuation of industrial agriculture. As agribusiness companies merge and expand, they exert more and more control on the world's agricultural resources. They also become more and more distant from the land, and financial concerns often overtake concerns about sustainability.

In 2007, for the first time in decades, a US census showed that the number of small farms

> "Since our existence is primarily dependent on farming, we cannot entrust this essential activity solely to the farming population—just 2 percent of Americans. As farming becomes more and more remote from the life of the average person, it becomes less and less able to provide us with clean, healthy, life-giving food or a clean, healthy, life-giving environment. A small minority of farmers, laden with debt and overburdened with responsibility, cannot possibly meet the needs of all the people."[2]
>
> — *Trauger M. Groh and Steven S. H. McFadden,*
> *authors of* Farms of Tomorrow

is on the rise.[3] Experts believe this is a response to the growing demand for local and organic food. As people are becoming more concerned about how their food is produced, family farmers are discovering a market for their locally and sustainably grown food. The number of farmers' markets has also been steadily increasing, offering places for people to buy fresh, healthful food from people in their own community. Farmers' markets foster close connections between farmers and those they serve. Farmers learn how to better meet the needs of their communities, and in return, communities help support and sustain their local farms.

Community-supported agriculture (CSA) is another current trend in supporting local small farms. Originating in the late twentieth century, CSA is a way for farms and communities to

SUSTAINING OUR OCEANS

A research project begun in Hawaii in 2011 seeks to revolutionize fish farming through new technology. Marine biologists are researching what they call an Aquapod that keeps farmed fish contained while letting them drift in the ocean, their natural habitat. The pod is a mesh enclosure that can drift at various depths in the sea. According to one participant in the project, this pod is harmless to the surrounding environment. Says Neil Anthony Sims, project participant and co-CEO of Kampachi Farms,

The fish are healthy, growing well, and are where they're meant to be—in the ocean. This technology has the potential to revolutionize fish farming, making it the most impact-free form of food production on the planet.[4]

share both the risks and benefits of farming. CSA farmers sell shares of their farm to members of the community. Those who buy these shares help cover the costs of running the farm and sometimes even do work on the farm. In return, they receive a share of the farm's crops each week. However, CSA members also share in the risks of their chosen farm. Whatever hardships the farmers experience are reflected in the shares of crops the members receive. If disease wipes out a farmer's crop of tomatoes, CSA members will not get tomatoes. CSA further strengthens the ties between farms and community, encouraging a local and sustainable approach to food in the future.

TOWARD A SUSTAINABLE FUTURE

Though the process of learning how to live sustainably in a dynamic world will never end, an increasing array of tools is becoming available to us. These technologies and innovations, along with an attitude of curiosity and concern, can help the new generation of sustainable farmers and consumers reach their goals.

Our curiosity will allow us to begin to understand the web of actions and reactions that ties us to Earth. If we are concerned enough to change our actions in order to encourage sustainable reactions, then we have hope of developing a system of agriculture that will make our planet resilient in the face of the challenges that lie ahead.

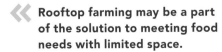

◀◀ Rooftop farming may be a part of the solution to meeting food needs with limited space.

GLOSSARY

AGRIBUSINESS—An industry engaged in farm related activities including farm operations, farm machinery, and farm product storage, transport, and sale.

AGROFORESTRY—The practice of growing trees along with crops for mutual benefit.

AQUAPONICS—The practice of raising fish in combination with growing crops.

BIODIVERSITY—Having a variety of plant and animal species in an environment.

CELLULOSE—A woody fiber found in plants.

CLIMATE CHANGE—A change in temperature and weather patterns due to human activity such as burning fossil fuels.

COMPOST—Decayed organic matter used to fertilize crops.

COVER CROP—A crop planted to prevent soil erosion, discourage the growth of weeds, and add organic matter or nutrients to the soil.

CROP ROTATION—The practice of alternating or switching crops grown on a given plot of land.

DEGRADATION—The act of wearing down or making worse.

GREENHOUSE GAS—A gas, such as carbon dioxide or methane, that contributes to global warming.

GROUNDWATER—Water within the earth that often supplies wells and springs.

INTERCROPPING—The practice of growing one crop between rows of another.

LEGUME—Any of a family of plants bearing nodules on the roots that contain nitrogen-fixing bacteria.

RESILIENT—Tending to recover from or adjust easily to misfortune or change.

RUNOFF—Rain or water that reaches streams or other bodies of water, often containing dissolved or floating material.

SUBSIDIES—Grants of money, often from the government.

SUSTAINABLE—Relating to a method of harvesting or using a resource so that the resource is not depleted or permanently damaged.

TRANSGENE—A gene from one species that has been incorporated into an organism or cell from a different species.

VERMICULTURE—The practice of using worms to make compost.

YIELD—The amount produced.

ADDITIONAL RESOURCES

SELECTED BIBLIOGRAPHY

2011 State of the World: Innovations that Nourish the Planet. New York: W. W. Norton, 2011. Print.

Francis, Charles A., et al., eds. *Developing and Extending Sustainable Agriculture: A New Social Contract.* New York: Haworth Food & Agricultural Products Press, 2006. Print.

Ikerd, John. "The Family Farm on the Cutting Edge." *John E. Ikerd.* University of Missouri, 27 May 2010. Web. 21 Nov. 2011.

McIntyre, Beverly D., et al. ed. *IAASTD Global Report: Agriculture at a Crossroads.* Washington, DC: Island Press, 2009. PDF.

Wiegandt, Klaus, ed. *Feeding the Planet: Environmental Protection through Sustainable Agriculture.* London: Haus, 2009. Print.

FURTHER READINGS

Fox, Thomas J. *Urban Farming: Sustainable City Living in Your Backyard, in Your Community, and in the World.* Irvine, CA: Hobby Farm/Bowtie, 2011. Print.

Leiner, Katherine. *Growing Roots: The New Generation of Sustainable Farmers, Cooks, and Food Activists.* Durango, CO: Sunrise Lane Productions, 2010. Print.

WEB LINKS

To learn more about sustainable agriculture, visit ABDO Publishing Company online at **www.abdopublishing.com**. Web sites about sustainable agriculture are featured on our Book Links page. These links are routinely monitored and updated to provide the most current information available.

FOR MORE INFORMATION

For more information on this subject, contact or visit the following organizations:

FOOD AND AGRICULTURE ORGANIZATION OF THE UNITED NATIONS (FAO)
Viale delle Terme di Caracalla, 00153 Rome, Italy
+3906-57051
http://www.fao.org/

FAO is an international organization devoted to finding a solution to world hunger. Contact them to find out what you can do to help fight hunger.

UNITED STATES DEPARTMENT OF AGRICULTURE (USDA)
1400 Independence Ave., S.W., Washington, DC 20250
202-720-2791
http://usda.gov/wps/portal/usda/usdahome

The USDA guides the United States government on issues relating to agriculture, including farming and food. Contact them for information about US policy on agriculture.

SOURCE NOTES

CHAPTER 1. FOOD FOR THOUGHT

1. "The World Factbook: World." *Central Intelligence Agency*. Central Intelligence Agency, 26 Oct. 2011. Web. 16 Aug. 2012.

2. Beverly D. McIntyre, et al. *IAASTD Global Report: Agriculture at a Crossroads*. Washington, DC: Island Press, 2009. PDF. 16 Aug. 2012.

3. *2011 State of the World: Innovations that Nourish the Planet*. New York: Norton, 2011. Print. xxiv–xxix.

4. John E. Ikerd. "The Family Farm on the Cutting Edge." *John E. Ikerd*. University of Missouri, 27 May 2010. Web. 16 Aug. 2012.

5. Joseph Fiksel. "Sustainability and Resilience: Toward a Systems Approach." *Sustainability: Science, Practice, and Policy* 2.2 (Fall 2006). PDF. 16 Aug. 2012.

CHAPTER 2. THE HISTORY OF AGRICULTURE

1. John L. Seitz and Kristen A. Hite. *Global Issues: An Introduction*. Chichester, UK: Wiley, 2012. *Google Book Search*. Web. 16 Aug. 2012.

CHAPTER 3. THE IMPORTANCE OF SUSTAINABLE AGRICULTURE

1. Ross W. Gorte and Pervaze A. Sheikh. "Deforestation and Climate Change." *Congressional Research Service*. Congressional Research Service, 24 Mar. 2010. Web. 16 Aug. 2012.

2. "'Energy-Smart' Agriculture Needed to Escape Fossil Fuel Trap." *Food and Agriculture Organization of the United Nations*. FAO, 29 Nov. 2011. Web. 16 Aug. 2012.

3. "The World Factbook: World." *Central Intelligence Agency*. Central Intelligence Agency, 26 Oct. 2011. Web. 16 Aug. 2012.

4. "Global Deforestation." *University of Michigan*. Regents of the University of Michigan, 4 Jan. 2010. Web. 16 Aug. 2012.

5. "The Tropical Rain Forest." *University of Michigan*. Regents of the University of Michigan, 6 Nov. 2008. Web. 16 Aug. 2012.

6. "Insecticide." *Encyclopaedia Britannica*. Encyclopaedia Britannica, 2012. Web. 16 Aug. 2012.

7. "Forests and Climate Change." *FAO Newsroom*. FAO, 27 Mar. 2006. Web. 16 Aug. 2012.

CHAPTER 4. THE NEED FOR SUSTAINABLE ENERGY

1. "Renewable Energy." *Encyclopaedia Britannica.* Encyclopaedia Britannica, 2012. Web. 16 Aug. 2012.

2. "'Energy-Smart' Agriculture Needed to Escape Fossil Fuel Trap." *Food and Agriculture Organization of the United Nations.* FAO, 29 Nov. 2011. Web. 16 Aug. 2012.

3. "The World Factbook: World." *Central Intelligence Agency.* Central Intelligence Agency, 26 Oct. 2011. Web. 16 Aug. 2012.

4. "Wind Power." *Encyclopaedia Britannica.* Encyclopaedia Britannica, 2012. Web. 16 Aug. 2012.

5. Ibid.

6. "Farming the Wind: Wind Power and Agriculture." *Union of Concerned Scientists.* Union of Concerned Scientists, 2012. Web. 16 Aug. 2012.

7. "Solar Energy Use in US Agriculture Overview and Policy Issues." *USDA.* US Department of Agriculture, Apr. 2011. PDF. 16 Aug. 2012.

8. "Reducing Food Miles." *National Sustainable Agriculture Information Service.* National Center for Appropriate Technology, 26 Apr. 2012. Web. 16 Aug. 2012.

9. "Clean Energy Farming." *SARE.* Sustainable Agriculture and Research Education, 2012. Web. 16 Aug. 2012.

10. Ibid.

11. "Biofuel." *Encyclopaedia Britannica.* Encyclopaedia Britannica, 2012. Web. 16 Aug. 2012.

12. Catherine Brahic. "Forget Biofuels—Burn Oil and Plant Forests Instead." *New Scientist.* Reed Business Information, 16 Aug. 2007. Web. 16 Aug. 2012.

13. "Biofuel." *Encyclopaedia Britannica.* Encyclopaedia Britannica, 2012. Web. 16 Aug. 2012.

14. "Clean Energy Farming." *SARE.* Sustainable Agriculture and Research Education, 2012. Web. 16 Aug. 2012.

15. N. B. McLaughlin, et al. "Comparison of Energy Inputs for Inorganic Fertilizer and Manure Based Corn Production." *Canadian Agricultural Engineering* 42.1 (2000). PDF. 16 Aug. 2012.

CHAPTER 5. BIOTECHNOLOGY AND GENETIC ENGINEERING

1. Beverly D. McIntyre, et al. *IAASTD Global Report: Agriculture at a Crossroads.* Washington, DC: Island Press, 2009. PDF. 16 Aug. 2012.

2. Klaus Wiegandt, ed. *Feeding the Planet: Environmental Protection through Sustainable Agriculture.* London: Haus, 2009. Print. 136–137.

3. Klaus Wiegandt, ed. *Feeding the Planet: Environmental Protection through Sustainable Agriculture.* London: Haus, 2009. Print. 137–139.

4. J. E. O. Rege. "Biotechnology Options for Improving Livestock in Developing Countries, with Special Reference to Sub-Saharan Africa." *FAO.* FAO, n.d. Web. 16 Aug. 2012.

CHAPTER 6. PRECISION AGRICULTURE

1. "Pesticide Air Initiative: Innovative Technologies—Precision Agriculture." *California Environmental Protection Agency Department of Pesticide Regulation.* State of California, n.d. PDF. 16 Aug. 2012.

2. Heather Haberman. "Groundfish Surveying." *NOAA Teacher at Sea Blog.* National Oceanic and Atmospheric Administration, 7 July 2011. Web. 16 Aug. 2012.

3. John Dietz. "Experience Aids Variable-Rate Technology." *Agriculture.com.* Meredith Corporation, 11 Jan. 2011. Web. 16 Aug. 2012.

4. "Our Community Food Center." *Growing Power.* Growing Power, n.d. Web. 16 Aug. 2012.

5. J. A. Ginsberg. "The Farm Next Door: Urban Agriculture, Biomimicry, Aquaponics, Why Worms Are Priceless & How Will Allen Aims to Fix the World." *News Tracker.* News Tracker, 26 Sept. 2009. Web. 16 Aug. 2012.

CHAPTER 7. BIODIVERSE FARMING SYSTEMS

1. Beverly D. McIntyre, et al. *IAASTD Global Report: Agriculture at a Crossroads.* Washington, DC: Island Press, 2009. PDF. 16 Aug. 2012.

2. Charles A. Francis, et al. *Developing and Extending Sustainable Agriculture: A New Social Contract.* New York: Haworth, 2006. Print. 29.

3. "Pest Resistant Crops." *GMO Compass.* GMO Compass, 22 Dec. 2006. Web. 16 Aug. 2012.

4. "What Is Sustainable Agriculture?" *SARE.* Sustainable Agriculture and Research Education, n.d. Web. 16 Aug. 2012.

5. "Empowering African Farmers to Eradicate *Striga* from Maize Croplands." *The African Agricultural Technology Foundation.* The African Agricultural Technology Foundation, 2006. PDF. 16 Aug. 2012.

6. Jan Piotrowski. "Fish and Rice Flourish Together in Paddies." *Nature.* Nature Publishing Group, 17 Nov. 2011. Web. 16 Aug. 2012.

CHAPTER 8. THE FUTURE OF SUSTAINABLE AGRICULTURE

1. "Cutting Food Waste to Feed the World." *Food and Agriculture Organization of the United Nations.* FAO, 2012. Web. 16 Aug. 2012.

2. Suzanne DeMuth. "Defining Community Supported Agriculture." *US Department of Agriculture National Agricultural Library.* USDA, Sept. 1993. Web. 16 Aug. 2012.

3. Steve King. "The Growth of Small Farms." *US News & World Report: Money.* US News & World Report, 25 Feb. 2009. Web. 16 Aug. 2012.

4. "'Velella' Research Project Promises to Revolutionize Sustainable Aquaculture." *PR Newswire.* PR Newswire, 14 Sept. 2011. Web. 16 Aug. 2012.

INDEX

ABOUT THE AUTHOR

Lisa Owings has a degree in English and creative writing from the University of Minnesota. She has written and edited a variety of educational books for children. Lisa lives in Andover, Minnesota, where her husband helps her tend a sustainable garden in their backyard.

ABOUT THE CONTENT CONSULTANT

Ryan Anderson is an assistant professor of Agriculture Education and Studies at Iowa State University. He is director of undergraduate education and an advisor for the Agricultural Education Club. He received his PhD from Virginia Polytechnic Institute and State University in Blacksburg, Virginia.